THE

WITCH-PERSECUTIONS

From TRANSLATIONS AND REPRINTS FROM THE
ORIGINAL SOURCES OF EUROPEAN HISTORY.

Edited by George L. Burr, A. B.

I

INTRODUCTION.

The belief in witchcraft and the persecution of those supposed to practice it have been almost universal in human history. Christianity inherited both the belief and the persecution from the religions, Jewish and pagan, which preceded it. But, under the influence of its monotheistic faith and its humane spirit, it was long before the belief became throughout Christendom a panic and the persecution an epidemic. When, however, in the thirteenth century, the scholastic theology, in its love of logical completeness, gave new prominence to the Devil and his followers as the counterpart and parody of God and his church and when, in the fourteenth century, the Holy Inquisition, successful in rooting out the heretics, turned its idle hands to the extirpation of those viler sinners whom it believed plighted wholly to Satan, the terror grew. The witch-persecutions it engendered ravaged for centuries all Christian lands, and have not yet wholly died away. It is with these persecutions, from their rise into full activity in the fifteenth century to their culmination in the seventeenth, that the present study deals. It seeks to illustrate their source, their scope, and their methods. With the superstitions which suggested the charges it concerns itself little. Both in these and in the procedure there is much too foul or too brutal for reproduction here. It was, indeed, no small part of the evil of the matter, that it so long debauched the imagination of Christendom.

I. THE THEORY OF WITCH-PERSECUTION.

Perhaps no better statement of the theory of witch-persecution, as it came to be accepted in all lands and by all shades of faith throughout Christendom, can anywhere be found than that of the Rev. Cotton Mather in a sermon which did much to make that theory known and effective in New England. The sermon, preached in Boston in 1689, was speedily printed, under the title of *A Discourse on Witchcraft*, in Mather's *Memorable Providences relating to Witchcraft and Possessions* (Boston, 1689). This book, "recommended by the Ministers of Boston and Charleston," was in no small degree responsible for the great Salem persecution, which broke out in 1692.

I. THE NATURE AND REALITY OF WITCHCRAFT.

Cotton Mather: Memorable Providences relating to Witchcrafts and Possessions (Boston, 1689), pp. 4-9 of "A Discourse on Witchcraft." English.

Such an Hellish thing there is as *Witchcraft* in the World. There are Two things which will be desired for the advantage of this Assertion. It should *first* be show'd,

WHAT *Witchcraft* is;

My Hearers will not expect from me an accurate *Definition* of the *vile Thing*; since the Grace of God has given me the Happiness to speak without *Experience* of it. But from Accounts both by *Reading* and *Hearing* I have learn'd to describe it so.

WITCHCRAFT is the Doing of *Strange* (and for the most part *Ill*) Things by the help of *evil Spirits, Covenanting* with (and usually *Representing* of) the woful children of men.

This is the *Diabolical Art* that *Witches* are notorious for.

4

First. *Witches* are the Doers of *Strange* Things. They cannot indeed perform any proper *Miracles*; those are things to be done only by the *Favourites* and *Embassadours* of the LORD. But *Wonders* are often produced by them, though chiefly such Wonders as the Apostle calls in 2. *Thes.* 2. 9. *Lying wonders.* There are *wonderful Storms* in the *great* World, and *wonderful Wounds* in the *little* World, [1] often effected by these *evil Causes.* They do things which transcend the ordinary *Course* of Nature, and which puzzle the ordinary *Sense* of Mankind. Some *strange* things are done by them in a way of *Real Production.* They do really *Torment*, they do really *Afflict* those that their Spite shall extend unto. Other *Strange* Things are done by them in a way of *Crafty Illusion.* They do craftily make of the *Air*, the *Figures* and *Colours* of things that never can be truly created by them. All men might *see*, but, I believe, no man could *feel*, some of the Things which the *Magicians* of *Egypt* exhibited of old.

Secondly. They are not only *strange* Things, but *Ill* Things, that *Witches* are the Doers of. In this regard also they are not the Authors of *Miracles*: those are things *commonly* done for the *Good* of Man, alwaies done for the *Praise* of *God.* But of these *Hell-hounds* it may in a special manner be said, as in *Psal.* 52, 3. *Thou lovest evil more than good.* For the most part they labour to robb *Man* of his *Ease* or his *Wealth*; they labour to wrong *God* of His *Glory.* There is Mention of Creatures that they call *White Witches*, which do only *Good-Turns* for their Neighbours. I suspect that there are none of that sort; but rather think, *There is none that doeth good, no, not one.* If they *do good*, it is only that they *may* do *hurt.*

Thirdly. It is by virtue of *evil Spirits* that *Witches* do what they do. We read in *Ephes.* 2, 2. about the *Prince of the power of the air.* There is confined unto the *Atmosphere* of our *Air* a vast *Power*, or *Army* of *Evil Spirits*, under the Government of a Prince

---

[1] i. e., in Man--the microcosm. The "great world" is the universe.

who employes them in a continual Opposition to the Designs of GOD: The Name of that *Leviathan*, who is the *Grand-Seigniour of Hell*, we find in the Scripture to be *Belzebub*. Under the Command of that mighty Tyrant, there are vast *Legions* & *Myriads* of Devils, whose *Businesses* & *Accomplishments* are not all the same. Every one has his *Post*, and his *Work*; and they are all glad of an opportunity to be mischievous in the World. These are they by whom *Witches* do exert their Devillish and malignant Rage upon their *Neighbours.* And especially Two Acts concur hereunto. The *First* is, Their *Covenanting* with the Witches. There is a most hellish *League* made between them, with various *Rites* and *Ceremonies.* The *Witches* promise to serve the *Devils*, and the *Devils* promise to *help* the witches; *How?* It is not convenient ² to be related. The *Second* is, their *Representing* of the Witches. And hereby indeed these are drawn into *Snares* and *Cords* of Death. The Devils, when they go upon the Errands of the *Witches*, do bear their *Names*; and hence do *Harmes* too come to be carried from the *Devils* to the *Witches*. We need not suppose such a wild thing as the *Transforming* of those Wretches into *Bruits* or *Birds*, as we too often do. It should next be proved *THAT* Witchcraft *is*.

The *Being* of such a thing is denied by many that place *a great part* of their *small wit* in derideing the Stories that are told of it. Their chief Argument is, That they never *saw* any Witches, therefore there are *none*. Just as if you or I should say, We never met with any *Robbers* on the Road, therefore there never was any *Padding* there.

Indeed the *Devils* are loath to have true Notions of *Witches* entertained with us. I have beheld them to put out the eyes of an enchaunted Child, when a Book that proves, *There is Witchcraft*, was laid before her. But there are especially Two Demonstrations that evince the Being of that Infernal mysterious thing.

---

² i. e., not seemly: perhaps because the details are too vile, perhaps because the preacher will not tempt his hearers.

First. We have the Testimony of *Scripture* for it. We find *Witchcrafts* often mentioned, sometimes by way of *Assertion,* sometimes by. way of *Allusion,* in the Oracles of God. Besides that, We have there the History of diverse *Witches* in these infallible and inspired Writings. Particularly, the Instance of the *Witch* at *Endor,* in I *Sam.* 28, 7. is so plain and full that *Witchcraft* it self is not a more amazing thing, than any *Dispute* about the Being of it, after this. The Advocates of *Witches* must use more *Tricks* to make Nonsense of the *Bible,* than ever the *Witch* of *Endor* used in her Magical Incantations, if they would evade the Force of that famous History. They that will believe no *Witches,* do imagine that *Jugglers* only are meant by them whom the Sacred Writ calleth so. But what do they think of that law in *Exod.* 22. 18. *Thou shalt not suffer a Witch to live?* Methinks 'tis a little too hard to punish every silly *Juggler* with so great Severity.

Secondly. We have the *Testimony* of *Experience* for it. What will those *Incredulous,* who must be the only Ingenious men, say to This? Many *Witches* have like those in Act. 19. 18. *Confessed and shewed their Deeds.* We see those things done, that it is impossible any Disease or any Deceit should procure. We see some hideous *Wretches* in hideous *Horrours* confessing, *That they did the Mischiefs.* This *Confession* is often made by them that are owners of as much Reason as the people that laugh at all *Conceit* of *Witchcraft*: the exactest Scrutiny of skilful Physicians cannot find any Distraction in their minds. This *Confession* is often made by them that are apart One from another, and yet they *agree* in all the Circumstances of it. This Confession is often made by them that at the same time will produce the *Engines* and *Ensignes* of their *Hellish Trade,* and give the standers-by an *Ocular Conviction* of *what* they do, and *how.* There can he no Judgment left of any *Humane Affairs,* if such *Confessions* must be Ridiculed: all the *Murders,* yea, and all the *Bargains* in the World must be meer *Imaginations* if such *Confessions* are of no Account.

2. THE DUTY OF PERSECUTION.

Bodin, De la Démonomanie des Sorciers, Paris, 1580 liv. iv, chap. 5. French.

Jean Bodin, jurist and statesman, was not only one of the most eminent European publicists of the sixteenth century, but one of the most rational and tolerant thinkers of his time. Yet even such a man could thus write "Of the punishments deserved by witches":

There are two means by which states are maintained in their weal and greatness--reward and penalty: the one for the good, the other for the bad. And, if the distribution of these two be faulty, nothing else is to be expected than the inevitable ruin of the state. . . .

But those greatly err who think that penalties are established only to punish crime. I hold that this is the least of the fruits which accrue therefrom to the state. For the greatest and the chief is the appeasing of the wrath of God, especially if the crime is directly against the majesty of God, as is this one. . . . Now, if there is any means to appease the wrath of God, to gain his blessing, to strike awe into some by the punishment of others, to preserve some from being infected by others, to diminish the number of evildoers, to make Secure the life of the well-disposed, and to punish the most detestable crimes of which the human mind can conceive, it is to punish with the utmost rigor the witches . . . .[3] Now, it is not within the power of princes to pardon a crime which the law of God punishes with the penalty of death--such as are the crimes of witches. Moreover, princes do gravely insult God in pardoning such horrible crimes committed directly against his majesty, seeing that the pettiest prince avenges with death

---

[3] Bodin then proceeds to enumerate fifteen distinct crimes, all horrid, of which every witch is guilty, and argues that, in default of proof, violent presumption should suffice for the sentence of witches to death.

insults against himself. Those too who let the witches escape, or who do not punish them with the utmost rigor, may rest assured that they will lie abandoned by God to the mercy of the witches. And the country which shall tolerate this will be scourged with pestilences, famines, and wars; and those which shall take vengeance on the witches will be blessed by him and will make his anger to cease. Therefore it is that one accused of being a witch ought never to be folly acquitted and set free unless the calumny of the accuser is clearer than the sun, inasmuch as the proof of such crimes is so obscure and so difficult that not one witch in a million would be accused or punished if the procedure were governed by the ordinary rules. . . .

II. THE BEGINNINGS OF THE

WITCH-PERSECUTIONS.

I. WITCH-PERSECUTION IN THE EARLIER FIFTEENTH CENTURY.

Nider, Formicarius, ed. of Augsburg, ca. 1476, lib. v, cap. 3. Latin.

One of the earliest books which throws light upon the methods of the persecutions is the *Formicarius*, or "Ant-Hill," of the Dominican theological professor, Johannes Nider, written, in its final form, about 1437. The work is an edifying dialogue between a theologian and a doubter as to sundry topics difficult to faith; and its fifth and final book is devoted to "witches and their deceptions." The sources and the nature of Nider's knowledge may be gathered from the following answer of the theologian to the doubter's request for information as to the injuries inflicted by witches upon the human beings.

I will relate to you some examples, which I have gained in part from the teachers of our faculty, in part from the experience of a certain upright secular judge, worthy of all faith, who from the torture and confession of witches and from his experiences in public and private has learned many things of this sort--a man with whom I have often discussed this subject broadly and deeply--to wit, Peter, a citizen of Bern, in the diocese of Lausanne, who has burned many Witches of both sexes, and has driven others out of the territory of the Bernese. [4] I have moreover conferred with one Benedict, a monk of the Benedictine order, who, although now a very devout cleric in a reformed monastery at Vienna, was a decade ago, while still in the world, a

---

[4] This Peter has been shown to be Peter of Gruyères, Bernese castellan in the Simmenthal, 1392-1406.

necromancer, juggler, buffoon, and strolling player, well-known as an expert among the secular nobility. I have likewise heard certain of the following things from the Inquisitor of Heretical Pravity [5] at Autun, who was a devoted reformer of our order in the convent at Lyons, and has convicted many of witchcraft in the diocese of Autun.

Relating then two or three anecdotes derived from these sources, the theologian closes his answer with this one:

The same procedure was more clearly described by another young man, arrested and burned as a witch, although, as I believe, truly, penitent, who had earlier, together with his wife, a witch invincible to persuasion, [6] escaped the clutches of the aforesaid judge, Peter. The aforesaid youth, being again indicted at Bern, with his wife, and placed in a different prison from hers, declared: "If I can obtain absolution for my sins, I will freely lay bare all I know about witchcraft, for I see that I have death to expect." And when he had been assured by the scholars that, if he should truly repent, he would certainly be able to gain absolution for his sins, then he gladly offered himself to death, and disclosed the methods of the primeval infection.

The ceremony, he said, of my seduction was as follows: First, on a Sunday, before the holy water is consecrated, the future disciple with his masters must go into the church, and there in their presence must renounce Christ and his faith, baptism, and the church universal. Then he must do homage to the *magisterulus*, that is, to the little master (for so, and not otherwise, they call the Devil). Afterward he drinks from the aforesaid flask; [7] and, this done, he forthwith feels himself to conceive and hold within himself an image of our art and the chief rites of this sect. After

---

[5] Such was the official title of a representative of the Holy inquisition.

[6] This means, of course, only that she could not be persuaded to confess.

[7] A flask described in a preceding anecdote as filled with a liquid made from murdered infants.

II

this fashion was I seduced; and my wife also, whom I believe of so great pertinacity that she will endure the flames rather than confess the least whit of the truth; but, alas, we are both guilty. What the young man had said was found in all respects the truth. For, after confession, the young man was seen to die in great contrition. His wife, however, though convicted by the testimony of witnesses, would not confess the truth even under the torture or in death; but, when the fire was prepared for her by the executioner, uttered in most evil words a curse upon him, and so was burned.

2. THE WITCH-BULL OF 1484.

Bullarium Romanum (Taurinensis editio), sub anno 1484. Latin. The bull is also printed in full at the head of the *Malleus maleficarum*, described below.

Despite the efforts of the Dominicans, it was with much difficulty that the new terror of witchcraft and the persecution based on it were spread throughout Europe. In Germany, especially, the Inquisitors charged with the task found themselves hampered by skepticism. In 1484, therefore, they turned their steps toward Rome for help, and on December 5th they won from the new Pope, Innocent VIII, a bull which once for all closed the mouths of doubters and compelled the coöperation of the German authorities, both ecclesiastical and lay. This bull, known from its first words as *Summis desiderantes*, runs as follows:

Innocentius, episcopus, servus servorum Dei. Ad futuram rei memoriam.

Desiring with supreme ardor, as pastoral solicitude requires, that the catholic faith in our days everywhere grow and flourish as much as possible, and that all heretical pravity be put far from the territories of the faithful, we freely declare and anew decree this by which our pious desire may be fulfilled, and, all errors being rooted out by our toil as with the hoe of a wise laborer, zeal and devotion to this faith may take deeper hold on the hearts of the faithful themselves.

It. has recently come to our ears, not without great pain to us, that in some parts of upper Germany, as well as in the provinces, cities, territories, regions, and dioceses of Mainz, Köln, Trier, Salzburg, and Bremen, many persons of both sexes, heedless of their own salvation and forsaking the catholic faith, give themselves over to devils male and female, and by their

13

incantations, charms, and conjurings, and by other abominable superstitions and sortileges, offences, crimes, and misdeeds, ruin and cause to perish the offspring of women, the foal of animals, the products of the earth, the grapes of vines, and the fruits of trees, as well as men and women, cattle and flocks and herds and animals of every kind, vineyards also and orchards, meadows, pastures, harvests, grains and other fruits of the earth; that they afflict and torture with dire pains and anguish, both internal and external, these men, women, cattle, flocks, herds, and animals, and hinder men from begetting and women from conceiving, and prevent all consummation of marriage; that, moreover, they deny with sacrilegious lips the faith they received in holy baptism; and that, at the instigation of the enemy of mankind, they do not fear to commit and perpetrate many other abominable offences and crimes, at the risk of their own souls, to the insult of the divine majesty and to the pernicious example and scandal of multitudes. And, although our beloved sons Henricus Institoris and Jacobus Sprenger, of the order of Friars Preachers, professors of theology, have been and still are deputed by our apostolic letters as inquisitors of heretical pravity, the former in the aforesaid parts of upper Germany, including the provinces, cities, territories, dioceses, and other places as above, and the latter throughout certain parts of the course of the Rhine; Nevertheless certain of the clergy and of the laity of those parts, seeking to be wise above what is fitting, because in the said letter of deputation the aforesaid provinces, cities, dioceses, territories, and other places, and the persons and offences in question were not individually and specifically named, do not blush obstinately to assert that these are not at all included in the said parts and that therefore it is illicit for the aforesaid inquisitors to exercise their office of inquisition in the provinces, cities, dioceses, territories, and other places aforesaid, and that they ought not to be permitted to proceed to the punishment, imprisonment, and correction of the aforesaid persons for the offences and crimes above named. Wherefore in the provinces, cities, dioceses, territories, and places aforesaid such offences and crimes, not without evident damage to their souls and risk of eternal salvation, go unpunished.

We therefore, desiring, as is our duty, to remove all impediments by which in any way the said inquisitors are hindered in the exercise of their office, and to prevent the taint of heretical pravity and of other like evils from spreading their infection to the ruin of others who are innocent, the zeal of religion especially impelling us, in order that the provinces, cities, dioceses, territories, and places aforesaid in the said parts of upper Germany may not be deprived of the office of inquisition which is their due, do hereby decree, by virtue of our apostolic authority, that it shall be permitted to the said inquisitors in these regions to exercise their office of inquisition and to proceed to the correction, imprisonment, and punishment of the aforesaid persons for their said offences and crimes, in all respects and altogether precisely as if the provinces, cities, territories, places, persons, and offences aforesaid were expressly named in the said letter. And, for the greater sureness, extending the said letter and deputation to the provinces, cities, dioceses, territories, places, persons, and crimes aforesaid, we grant to the said inquisitors that they or either of them, joining with them our beloved son Johannes Gremper, cleric of the diocese of Constance, master of arts, their present notary, or any other notary public who by them or by either of them shall have been temporarily delegated in the provinces, cities, dioceses, territories, and places aforesaid, may exercise against all persons, of whatsoever condition and rank, the said office of inquisition, correcting, imprisoning, punishing, and chastising, according to their deserts, those persons whom they shall find guilty as aforesaid.

And they shall also have full and entire liberty to propound and preach to the faithful the word of God, as often as it shall seem to them fitting and proper, in each and all of the parish churches in the said provinces, and to do all things necessary and suitable under the aforesaid circumstances, and likewise freely and fully to carry them out.

And moreover we enjoin by apostolic writ on our venerable brother, the Bishop of Strasburg, that, either in his own person or through some other or others solemnly publishing the foregoing wherever, whenever, and how often soever he may deem expedient or by these inquisitors or either of them may be legitimately required, he permit them not to be molested or hindered in any manner whatsoever by any authority whatsoever in the matter of the aforesaid and of this present letter, threatening all opposers, hinderers, contradicters, and rebels, of whatever rank, state, decree, eminence, nobility, excellence, or condition they may be, and whatever privilege of exemption they may enjoy, with excommunication, suspension, interdict, and other still more terrible sentences, censures, and penalties, as may be expedient, and this without appeal and with power after due process of law of aggravating and reaggravating these penalties, by our authority, as often as may be necessary, to this end calling in the aid, if need be, of the secular arm.

And this, all other apostolic decrees and earlier decisions to the contrary notwithstanding; or if to any, jointly or severally, there has been granted by this apostolic see exemption from interdict, suspension, or excommunication, by apostolic letters not making entire, express, and literal mention of the said grant of exemption; or if there exist any other indulgence whatsoever, general or special, of whatsoever tenor, by failure to name which or to insert it bodily in the present letter the carrying out of this privilege could be hindered or in any way put off, or any of whose whole tenor special mention must be made in our letters. Let no man, therefore, dare to infringe this page of our declaration, extension, grant, and mandate, or with rash hardihood to contradict it. If any presume to attempt this, let him know that he incurs the wrath of almighty God and of the blessed apostles Peter and Paul. [8]

Given in Rome, at St. Peter's, in the year of Our Lord's incarnation 1484, on the nones of December, in the first year of our pontificate.

---

[8] These "final clauses" are those found at this period in all bulls of the class known as *tituli*.

3. THE WITCH-HAMMER.

Even when armed with the papal bull, the German Inquisitors found their preparation incomplete. Soon after their return from Rome they set themselves at the compilation of a hand-book which should leave no judge an excuse for laxity--an exposition of witchcraft and a code of procedure for the detection and punishment of witches. This, completed in 1486, they called Malleus Maleficarum, "The Witch-Hammer." As a specimen may serve a part of its

Directions for the Torture of a Witch.

Malleus Maleficarum, pars iii, quæstio 14. Latin. Editions are many.

The method of beginning an examination by torture is as follows: First, the jailers prepare the implements of torture, then they strip the prisoner (if it be a woman, she has already been stripped by other women, upright and of good report). [9] This stripping is lest some means of witchcraft may have been sewed into the clothing--such as often, taught by the Devil, they prepare from the bodies of unbaptized infants, [murdered] that they may forfeit salvation. And when the implements of torture have been prepared, the judge, both in person and through other good men zealous in the faith, tries to persuade the prisoner to confess the truth freely; but, if he will not confess, he bids attendants make the prisoner fast to the strappado or some other implement of torture. The attendants obey forthwith, yet with feigned agitation. Then, at the prayer of some of those present, the prisoner is loosed again and is taken aside and once more persuaded to confess, being led to believe that be will in that case not be put to death.

---

[9] Sometimes, in place of the prisoner's clothing, a garment furnished by the court was now supplied, to be worn during the torture.

Here it may be asked whether the judge, in the case of a prisoner much defamed, convicted both by witnesses and by proofs, nothing being lacking but his own confession, can properly lead him to hope that his life will be spared--when, even if he confess his crime, he will be punished with death.

It must be answered that opinions vary. Some hold that even a witch of very ill repute, against whom the evidence justifies violent suspicion, and who, as a ringleader of the witches, is accounted very dangerous, may be assured her life, and condemned instead to perpetual imprisonment on bread and water, in case she will give sure and convincing testimony against other witches; yet this penalty of perpetual imprisonment must not be announced to her, but only that her life will be spared, and that she will be punished in some other fashion, perhaps by exile. And doubtless such notorious witches, especially those who prepare witch-potions or who by magical methods cure those bewitched, would be peculiarly suited to be thus preserved, in order to aid the bewitched or to accuse other witches, were it not that their accusations cannot be trusted, since the Devil is a liar, unless confirmed by proof and witnesses. Others hold, as to this point, that for a time the promise made to the witch sentenced to imprisonment is to be kept, but that after a time she should be burned.

A third view is, that the judge may safely promise witches to spare their lives, if only he will later excuse himself from pronouncing the sentence and will let another do this in his place. . . .

But if, neither by threats nor by promises such as these, the witch can be induced to speak the truth, then the jailers must carry out the sentence, and torture the prisoner according to the accepted methods, with more or less of severity as the delinquent's crime may demand. And, while he is being tortured, he must be questioned on the articles of accusation, and this frequently and persistently, beginning with the lighter charges--for he will more readily confess the lighter than the heavier. And, while this is being done, the notary must write down everything in his record of the trial--how the prisoner is tortured, on what points he is questioned, and how he answers.

And note that, if he confesses under the torture, he must afterward be conducted to another place, that he may confirm it and certify that it was not due alone to the force of the torture.

But, if the prisoner will not confess the truth satisfactorily, other sorts of tortures must be placed before him, with the statement that, unless he will confess the truth, he must endure these also. But, if not even thus be can be brought into terror and to the truth, then the next day or the next but one is to be set for a *continuation* of the torture--not a repetition, [10] for they must not be repeated unless new evidences be produced.

The judge must then address to the prisoners the following sentence: We, the judge, etc., do assign to you,------, such and such a day for the continuation of the tortures, that from your own mouth the truth may be heard, and that the whole may be recorded by the notary.

And during the interval, before the day assigned, the judge, in person or through approved men, must in the manner above described try to persuade the prisoner to confess, promising her [11] (if there is aught to be gained by this promise) that her life shall be spared.

The judge shall see to it, morever, that throughout this interval guards are constantly with the prisoner, so that she may not be

---

[10] This was, of course, a legal fiction, to avoid the merciful restriction put by law upon the repetition of torture.

[11] This change in the gender of the pronoun is a faithful following of the original.

left alone; because she will be visited by the Devil and tempted into suicide.

III. THE WITCH-PERSECUTION AT TRIER.

It was, however, not till a century later, in the second half of the sixteenth century, that the witch-persecutions reached their height. One of the fiercest was that which raged in the dominions of the Elector-Archbishop of Trier (Trèves) in western Germany. One who had been an eye-witness, the canon Linden, in later years described it thus:

I. THE SCOPE OF THE PERSECUTION.

Linden, *Gesta Trevirorum* (from his manuscript in the City Library of Trier.) [12] Latin.

Inasmuch as it was popularly believed that the continued sterility of many years was caused by witches through the malice of the Devil, the whole country rose to exterminate the witches. This movement was promoted by many in office, who hoped wealth from the persecution. And so, from court to court throughout the towns and villages of all the diocese, scurried special accusers, inquisitors, notaries, jurors, judges, constables, dragging to trial and torture human beings of both sexes and burning them in great numbers. Scarcely any of those who were accused escaped punishment or were there spared even the leading men in the city of Trier. For the Judge, [13] with two Burgomasters, several Councilors and Associate Judges, canons of sundry collegiate churches, parish-priests, rural deans, were swept away in this ruin. So far, at length, did the madness of the furious populace and of the courts go in this thirst for blood and booty that there was

---

[12] Printed in Hontheim's *Historia Trevirensis diplomatica* (iii, p. 170, note) and in Wyttenbach and Müller's ed. of the *Gesta Trevirorum*; but with more care in Burr, *The Fate of Dietrich Flade*.

[13] Dr. Dietrich Flade, judge of the secular court at Trier and deputy governor of the city, was perhaps the most eminent victim of the witch-persecution in Germany. It is probable that he owed his fate in part or wholly to his attempt to check the persecution. Tortured into confession, he was burned in 1589.

scarcely anybody who was not smirched by some suspicion of this crime.

Meanwhile notaries, copyists, and innkeepers grew rich. The executioner rode a blooded horse, like a noble of the court, and went clad in gold and silver; his wife vied with noble dames in the richness of her array. The children of those convicted and punished were sent into exile; their goods were confiscated; plowman and vintner failed-- hence came sterility. A direr pestilence or a more ruthless invader could hardly have ravaged the territory of Trier than this inquisition and persecution without bounds: many were the reasons for doubting that all were really guilty. This persecution lasted for several years; and some of those who presided over the administration of justice gloried in the multitude of the stakes, at each of which a human being had been given to the flames.

At last, though the flames were still unsated, the people grew impoverished, rules were made and enforced restricting the fees and costs of examinations and examiners, and suddenly, as when in war funds fail, the zeal of the persecutors died out.

2. THE RECANTATION OF LOOS.

Delrio, Disquisitiones Magicae, lib. v, appendix I. Latin.

It was during this persecution at Trier that Comelius Loos, a scholar of Dutch birth who held a professorship in the university of that city, dared to protest against both the persecution itself and the superstitions out of which it grew. Failing in his appeals to the authorities, he wrote a book to set forth his views; but the manuscript was seized in the hands of the printer, and Loos himself thrown into prison. Thence he was brought out, in the spring Of 1593, and, before the assembled church dignitaries of the place, pronounced a solemn recantation. This recantation has been preserved by the Jesuit Delrio in the great work which in

1599-1600 he published in support of the persecution. Thus Delrio tells the story:

And, finally, as I have made mention of Losæus Callidius, who tried by a thousand arts to make public the book which he had written in defence of the witches (and some fear that even yet some evil demon may bring this about), I have brought for an antidote the Recantation signed by him. Its authentic and so-called original copy is in the possession of a devout and most honorable man, Joannes Baxius, J. U. Lie. (whose energy and zeal against this nefarious heresy God will some day reward), from whom I have received the following transcript, certified by a notary:

I, Cornelius Losæus Callidius, born at the town of Gouda in Holland, but now (on account of a certain treatise On Trite and False Witchcraft, [14] rashly and presumptuously written without the knowledge and permission of the superiors of this place, shown by me to others, and then sent to be printed at Cologne) arrested and imprisoned in the Imperial Monastery of St. Maximin, near Trier, by order of the Most Reverend and Most Illustrious Lord, the Papal Nuncio, Octavius, Bishop of Tricarico: whereas I am informed of a surety that in the aforesaid book and also in certain letters of mine on the same subject sent clandestinely to the clergy and town council of Trier, and to others (for the purpose of hindering the execution of justice against the witches, male and female), are contained many articles which are not only erroneous and scandalous, but also suspected of heresy and smacking of the crime of treason, as being seditious and foolhardy, against the common opinion of decisions and bulls of theological teachers and the decisions and bulls of the Supreme Pontiffs, and contrary to the practice and to the statutes and laws of the magistrates and judges, not only of this Archdiocese of Trier, but of other provinces and principalities, I do therefore revoke, condemn,

---

[14] This book, confiscated by the ecclesiastical authorities, has been partly recovered in our own day.

reject, and repudiate the said articles, in the order in which they are here subjoined.

I. In the first place, I revoke, condemn, reject, and censure the idea (which both in words and writing I have often and before many persons pertinaciously asserted, and which I wished to be the head and front of this my disputation) that the things which are written about the bodily transportation or translation of witches, male and female, are altogether fanciful and must be reckoned the empty superstition; [and this I recant] both because it smacks of rank heresy and because this opinion partakes of sedition and hence savors of the crime of treason.

2. For (and this in the second place I recant), in the letters which I have clandestinely sent to sundry persons, I have pertinaciously, without solid reasons, alleged against the magistracy that the [aerial] flight of witches is false and imaginary; asserting, moreover, that the wretched creatures are compelled by the severity of the torture to confess things which they have never done, and that by cruel butchery innocent blood is shed and by a new alchemy gold and silver coined from human blood.

3. By these and by other things of the same sort, partly in private conversations among the people, partly in sundry letters addressed to both the magistracies, [15] I have accused of tyranny to their subjects the superiors and the judges.

4. And consequently, inasmuch as the Most Reverend and Most Illustrious Archbishop and Prince-Elector of Trier not only permits witches, male and female, to be subjected in his diocese to deserved punishment, but has also ordained laws regulating the method and costs of judicial procedure against witches, I have with heedless temerity tacitly insinuated the charge of tyranny against the aforesaid Elector of Trier.

---

[15] i. e. both lay and spiritual.

5. I revoke and condemn, moreover, the following conclusions of mine, to wit: that there are no witches who renounce God, pay worship to the Devil, bring storms by the Devils aid, and do other like things, but that all these things are dreams.

6. Also, that magic (*magia*) ought not to he called witchcraft (*maleficium*), nor magicians (*magi*) witches (*malefici*), and that the passage of Holy Scripture, "Thou shalt not suffer a witch to live" (*Maleficos non patieris vivere*), [16] is to be understood of those who by a natural use of natural poisons inflict death.

7. That no compact does or can exist between the Devil and a human being.

8. That devils do not assume bodies.

9. That the life of Hilarion written by St. Jerome is not authentic.

10. That there is no sexual intercourse between the Devil and human beings.

11. That neither devils nor witches can raise tempests, rainstorms, hail-storms, and the like, and that the things said about these are mere dreams.

12. That spirit and form apart from matter cannot be seen by man.

13. That it is rash to assert that whatever devils can do, witches also can do through their aid.

---

[16] Exodus, xxii, 18.

14. That the opinion that a superior demon can cast out an inferior is erroneous and derogatory to Christ. [17]

15. That the Popes in their bulls do not say that magicians and witches perpetrate such things (as are mentioned above).

16. That the Roman Pontiffs granted the power to proceed against witches, lest if they should refuse they might be unjustly accused of magic, just as some of their predecessors had been justly accused of it.

These assertions, all and singular, with many calumnies, falsehoods, and sycophancies, toward the magistracy, both secular and ecelesiastical, spitefully, immodestly, and falsely poured forth, without cause, with which my writings on magic teem, I hereby expressly and deliberately condemn, revoke, and reject, earnestly beseeching the pardon of God and of my superiors for what I have done, and solemnly promising that in future I will neither in word nor in writing, by myself or through others, in whatsoever place it may befall me to be, teach, promulgate, defend, or assert any of these things. If I shall do to the contrary, I subject myself thenceforward, as if it were now, to all the penalties of the law against relapsed heretics, recusants, seditious offenders, traitors, backbiters, sycophants, who have been openly convicted, and also to those ordained against perjurers. I submit myself also to arbitrary correction, whether by the Archbishop of Trier or by any other magistrates under whom it may befall me to dwell, and who may he certified of my relapse and of my broken faith, that they may punish me according to my deserts, in honor and reputation, property and person.

In testimony of all which I have, with my own hand, signed this my recantation of the aforesaid articles, in presence of notary and witnesses.

---

[17] A marginal note here cites Luke, xi.

(*Signed*)

CORNELIUS LOOSÆUS CALLIDIUS.

(*and attested*)

Done in the Imperial Monastery of St. Maximin, outside the walls of Trier, in the abbot's chamber, in presence of the Reverend, Venerable, and Eminent Sirs, Peter Binsfeld, [18] Bishop of Azotus, vicar-general in matters spiritual of the Most Reverend Archbishop of Trier, our most element lord, and Reinerus, abbot of the said monastery, Bartholomæus van Bodeghem, of Delft, J. U. L., Official of the Ecclesiastical Court of Trier, Georgius von Helffenstein, Doctor of Theology, Dean of the Collegiate Church of St. Simeon in the city of Trier, and Joannes Colmann, J. U. D., Canon of the said church and Seal-Bearer of the Court of Trier, [19] etc., in the year of Our Lord 1592 *more Trev.*, [20] on Monday, March 15th, in the presence of me the notary undersigned and of the worthy Nicolaus Dolent and Daniel Maier, secretary and copyist respectively of the Reverend Lord Abbot, as witnesses specially called and summoned to this end.

(*Signed*)

ADAMUS HEC Tectonius, Notary,

(*And below*)

---

[18] Binsfeld, suffragan bishop and real head of ecclesiastical affairs in the diocese, was doubtless the prime mover in the punishment of Loos. He had himself written a book, *De confessionibus maleficorum et sagarum* (Trier, 1589), to prove that the confessions of witches were worthy of all faith.

[19] i. e., the ecclesiastical court, of which Bodeghem was the head (the Official).

[20] 1593, according to our calendar; according to the *mos Trevirense* the year began on March 25th.

Compared with its original and found to agree, by me the undersigned Secretary of the town of Antwerp,

G. KIEFFEL.

Here you have the Recantation in full. And yet afterwards again at Brussels, while serving as curate in the church of Notre Dame de la Chapelle, he was accused of relapse, and was released only after a long imprisonment, and being again brought into suspicion (whence you way understand the pertinacity of his madness) escaped a third indictment through a premature death; but (much the pity!) left behind not a few partisans, men so imperfectly versed in medicine and sound theology as to share this stupid error. Would that they might he wise, and seriously realize at last how rash and noxious it is to prefer the ravings of a single heretic, Weyer, [21] to the judgment of the Church!

---

[21] Johann Weyer was a German physician, who in 1563 put forth a book attacking the witch-persecution. Loos had been influenced by this and was looked on as Weyer's disciple.

IV. THE WITCH-PERSECUTION AT BONN.

An undated letter [22] from the pastor (Duren) of the village of Alfter, near Bonn, to Count Werner of Salm thus describes the persecution in that city:

Those burned are mostly male witches of the sort described. There must be half the city implicated: for already professors, law-students, pastors, canons, vicars, and monks have here been arrested and burned. His Princely Grace has seventy wards [23] who are to become pastors, one of whom, eminent as a musician, was yesterday arrested; two others were sought for, but have fled. The Chancellor and his wife and the Private Secretary's wife are already executed. On the eve of Out Lady's Day there was executed here a maiden of nineteen who bore the name of being the fairest and the most blameless of all the city, and who from her childhood had been brought up by the Bishop himself A canon of the cathedral, named Rotenhahn, I saw beheaded and burned. Children of three or four years have devils for their paramours. Students and boys of noble birth, of nine, ten, eleven, twelve, thirteen, fourteen years, have here been burned. In fine, things are in such a pitiful state that one does not know with what people one may talk and associate.

---

[22] At least, the date of the letter is not given by W. v. Waldbrühl, who prints from it this extract in his *Naturforschung* and *Hexenglaube*, (Berlin, 1867). He says only that it had shortly before been found in the Salm archives. It belongs, doubtless, to the early seventeenth century. Bonn, not then a university town, was the official residence of the Prince-Archbishops of Cologne.

[23] Boys to be trained for priests in his seminary.

V. THE WITCH-PERSECUTION IN SCOTLAND.

From the contemporary pamphlet *Newes from Scotland*, 1591, as reprinted in Pitcairn's *Criminal Trials in Scotland*, vol. I, pt. 2, pp. 215-223. English.

Within the towne of Trenent, in the kingdome of Scotland, there dwelleth one David Seaton, who, being deputie bailiffe in the said towne, had a maid called Geillis Duncane, who used secretlie to absent and lie forth of hir maister's house every other night: This Geillis Duncane tooke in hand to helpe all such as were troubled or grieved with anie kinde of sicknes or infirmitie, and in short space did perfourme many matters most miraculous; which things, for asmuche as she began to do them upon a sodaine, having never done the like before, made her maister and others to be in great admiration, and wondered thereat: by means whereof, the saide Davide Seaton had his maide in great suspition that shee did not those things by naturall and lawful waies, but rather supposed it to bee done by some extraordinarie and unlawfull meanes. Whereupon, her maister began to grow verie inquisitive, and examined hir which way and by what means shee was able to performe matters of so great importance; whereat shee gave him no aunswere: nevertheless, her maister, to the intent that hee might the better trie and finde out the truth of the same, did with the help of others torment her with the torture of the pilliwinkes [24] upon her fingers, which is a grievous torture; and binding or wrinching her head with a cord or roape, which is a most cruell torment also; yet would she not confess anie thing; whereuppon, they suspecting that she had beene marked by the Devill (as commonly witches are), made diligent search about her, and found the enemies mark to be in her fore crag, or fore part of her throate; which being found, she confessed that al her doings was done by the wicked allurements and entisements of the Devil, and that she did them by witchcraft. After this her confession, she

---

[24] An instrument of torture similar to the thumbscrews later in use.

was committed to prison, where shee continued a season, where immediately shee accused these persons following to bee notorious witches, and caused them forthwith to be apprehended, one after another, viz. Agnes Sampson the eldest witche of them all, dwelling in Haddington; Agnes Tompson of Edenbrough [25]; Doctor Fian alias John Cuningham, master of the schoole at Saltpans in Lowthian, of whose life and strange acts you shal heare more largely in the end of this discourse. These were by the saide Geillis Duncane accused, as also George Motts wife, dwelling in Lowthian; Robert Grierson, skipper; and Jannet Blandilands; with the potter's wife of Seaton: the smith at the Brigge Hallis, with innumerable others in those parts, and dwelling in those bounds aforesaid; of whom some are alreadie executed, the rest remaine in prison to receive the doome of judgment at the Kinges Majesties will and pleasure.

The saide Geillis Duncane also caused Ewphame Mecalrean to bee apprehended, who conspired and performed the death of her godfather, and who used her art upon a gentleman, being one of the Lordes and Justices of the Session, for bearing good will to her daughter. Shee also caused to be apprehended one Barbara Naper, for bewitching to death Archibalde lait Earle of Angus, who languished to death by witchcraft, and yet the same was not suspected; but that bee died of so straunge a disease as the Phisition knewe not how to cure or remedie the same. But of all other the said witches, these two last before recited, were reputed for as civill honest women as anie that dwelled within the cittie of Edenbrough, before they were apprehended. Many other besides were taken dwelling in Lieth, [26] who are detayned in prison untill his Majesties further will and pleasure be knowne . . . . [27]

As touching the aforesaide Doctor Fian alias John Cunningham, the examination of his actes since his apprehension, declareth the

---

[25] Edinburgh.

[26] Leith.

[27] Then follows an account of the torture and confession of Agnes Sampson.

great subteltie of the Divell, and therefore maketh thinges to appeare the more miraculous; for beeing apprehended by the accusation of the saide Geillis Duncane aforesaide, who confessed he was their Regester, and that there was not one man suffered to come to the Divels readinges but onely hee: the saide Doctor was taken and imprisoned, and used with the accustomed paine provided for those offences, inflicted upon the rest, as is aforsaide. First, By thrawing of his head with a rope, whereat be would confesse nothing. Secondly, Hee was perswaded by faire meanes to confesse his follies, but that would prevaile as little. Lastly, Hee was put to the most severe and cruell paine in the worlde, called the bootes; [28] who after he had received three strokes, being inquired if he would confesse his damnable actes and wicked life, his toong would not serve him to speake; in respect whereof the rest of the witches willed to searche his toong, under which was founde two pinnes, thrust up into the heade; whereupon the witches did say, Now is the charme stinted; and shrewed, that those charmed pinnes were the cause he could not confesse any thing: Then was he immediately released of the bootes, brought before the King, [29] his confession was taken, and his own hand willingly set thereunto. . . . . [30]

---

[28] "The boots, or *bootikins*," says Pitcairn in his note on this passage, "were chiefly made use of in extreme cases, such as High Treason, Witchcraft, etc. This horrid instrument extended from the ankles to the knee, and at each stroke of a large hammer (which forced the wedges closer), the question was repeated. In many instances, the bones and flesh of the leg were crushed and lacerated in a shocking manner before confession was made."

[29] The personal interest taken in these trials by King James is explained by the fact that one of the crimes which the witches were made to confess was that they had gone to sea in sieves and there raised the contrary wind which distressed His Majesty's ship on his return from Denmark, whither he had gone to fetch his bride. It was, perhaps, the experience thus gained in the persecution which impelled King James later to compose a book on witchcraft (*Daemonologie*, Edinburgh, 1597); and which led him, on his ascent of the English throne in 1603, not only to bring out at London a fresh edition of this treatise, but to inspire a new and sterner English statute against the witches.

Thus, all the daie, this Doctor Fian continued very solitarie, and seemed to have a care of his owne soule, and would call uppon God, shewing himselfe penitent for his wicked life; nevertheless, the same night, hee found such meanes that he stole the key of the prison doore and chamber in which he was, which in the night bee opened and fled awaie to the Saltpans, where hee was alwayes resident, and first apprehended. Of whose sodaine departure, when the Kings Majestie had intelligence, hee presently commanded diligent inquirie to bee made for his apprehension; and for the better effecting thereof, hee sent publike proclamations into all partes of his lande to the same effect. By meanes, of whose hot and harde pursuite he was agayn taken, and brought to prison; and then, being called before the Kings Highnes, hee was re-examined, as well touching his departure, as also touching all that had before happened. But this Doctor, notwithstanding that his owne confession appeareth, remaining in recorde under his owne hande writting, and the same thereunto fixed in the presence of the Kings Majestic and sundrie of his Councell, yet did he utterly denie the same.

Whereupon the Kings Majestie, perceiving his stubborne willfulnesse, conceived and imagined, that in the time of his absence, hee had entered into newe conference and league with the Devill his maister; and that bee had beene again newly marked, for the which he was narrowly searched; but it coulde not in anie waie be founde; yet for more tryall of him, to make him confesse, bee was commaunded to have a most strange torment, which was done in this manner following. His nailes upon all his fingers were riven and pulled off with an instrument called in Scottish a Turkas, which in England wee call a payre of pincers, and under every nayle there was thrust in two needels over even

---

Under this statute of James was carried on the later witch-persecution in England; and it formed a basis for that in the colonies.

[30] Then follows a summary of his confession and an account of his commission to a solitary cell. What is next printed above is alleged to have happened on the morrow.

up to the heads. At all which torments notwithstanding, the Doctor never shronke anie whit; neither woulde he then confesse it the sooner, for all the tortures inflicted upon him. Then was hee, with all convenient speede, by commandement, convaied againe to the torment of the bootes, wherein hee continued a long time, and did abide so many blowes in them, that his legges were crusht and beaten together as small as might be; and the bones and flesh so brused, that the blond and marrow spouted forth in great abundance; whereby, they were made unserviceable for ever. And notwithstanding all these grievous paines and cruell torments, he would not confesse anie things; so deeply had the Devill entered into his heart, that bee utterly denied all that which he before avouched; and would saie nothing thereunto, but this, that what hee had done and sayde before, was onely done and sayde, for fear of paynes which he had endured.

Upon great consideration, therefore, taken by the Kings Majestie and his Councell, as well for the due execution of justice uppon such detestable malefactors, as also for example sake, to remayne a terror to all others heerafter, that shall attempt to deale in the lyke wicked and ungodlye actions as witchcraft, sorcerie, conjuration, and such lyke; the saide Doctor Fian was soon after arraigned, condemned and adjudged by the law to die, and then to be burned according to the lawe of that lande provided in that behalfe. Whereupon hee was put into a carte, and beeing first strangled, bee was immediately put into a great fire, being readie provided for that purpose, and there burned in the Castle Hill of Edenbrough, on a Saterdaie, in the ende of Januarie last past, 1591.

VI. THE

WITCH-PERSECUTION

AT BAMBERG.

From mss. in the Bamberg library, as printed by Leitschuh, Beiträge zur Geschichte des Hexenwesens in Franken (Bamberg, 1883).

In 1628 there was tried for witchcraft at the episcopal city of Bamberg, in Germany, the Burgomaster Johannes Junius. The minutes of the trial, which is in all respects a fair specimen of German witch-trials, are still to be seen at Bamberg. Translated from German into English, the greater part runs as follows:

... On Wednesday, June 28, 1628, was examined without torture Johannes Junius, Burgomaster at Bamberg, on the charge of witchcraft: how and in what fashion he had fallen into that vice. Is fifty-five years old, and was born at Niederwaysich in the Wetterau. Says he is wholly innocent, knows nothing of the crime, has never in his life renounced God; says that he is wronged before God and the world, would like to hear of a single human being who has seen him at such gatherings [as the witch-sabbaths].

Confrontation of Dr. Georg Adam Haan. Tells him to his face he will stake his life on it [er wolle darauf leben und sterben], that he saw him, Junius, a year and a half ago at a witch-gathering in the electoral council-room, where they ate and drank. Accused denies the same wholly.

Confronted with Hopffens Elsse. Tells him likewise that he was on Haupts-moor at a witch-dance; but first the holy wafer was desecrated. Junius denies. Hereupon he was told that his

36

accomplices had confessed against him and was given time for thought.

On Friday, June 30, 1628, the aforesaid Junius was again without torture exhorted to confess, but again confessed nothing, whereupon, . . . since he would confess nothing, he was put to the torture, and first the *Thumb-screws* were applied. Says he has never denied God his Saviour nor suffered himself to be otherwise baptized;[31] will again stake his life on it; feels no pain in the thumb-screws.

Leg-screws. Will confess absolutely nothing; knows nothing about it. He has never renounced God; will never do such a thing; has never been guilty of this vice; feels likewise no pain.

Is stripped and examined; on his right side is found a bluish mark, like a clover leaf, is thrice pricked therein, but feels no pain and no blood flows out.

Strappado. He has never renounced God, God will not forsake him; if be were such a wretch he would not let himself be so tortured; God must show some token of his innocence. He knows nothing about witchcraft. . . .

On July 5, the above named Junius is without torture, but with urgent persuasions, exhorted to confess, and at last begins and confesses:

When in the year 1624 his law-suit at Rothweil cost him some six hundred florins, he had gone out, in the month of August, into his orchard at Friedrichsbronnen; and, as he sat there in thought, there had come to him a woman like a grass-maid, who had asked him why he sat there so sorrowful; he had answered that he was not despondent, but she had led him by seductive

---

[31] "Otherwise baptized" is the usual phrase for the rite, a parody of baptism, by which the Devil was believed to initiate his followers.

speeches to yield him to her will. . . . And thereafter this wench had changed into the form of a goat, which bleated and said, "Now you see with whom you have had to do. You must be mine or I will forthwith break your neck." Thereupon be had been frightened, and trembled all over for fear. Than the transformed spirit had seized him by the throat and demanded that he should renounce God Almighty, whereupon Junius said, "God forbid," and thereupon the spirit vanquished through the power of these words. Yet it came straightway back, brought more people with it, and persistently demanded of him that he renounce God in Heaven and all the heavenly host, by which terrible threatening he was obliged to speak this formula. "I renounce God in Heaven and his host. and will henceforward recognize the Devil as my God."

After the renunciation he was so far persuaded by those present and by the evil spirit that he suffered himself to be otherwise baptized' in the evil spirit's name. The Morhauptin had given him a ducat as dower-gold, which afterward became only a potsherd.

He was then named Krix. His paramour he had to call Vixen. Those present had congratulated him in Beelzebub's name and said that they were now all alike. At this baptism of his there were among others the aforesaid Christiana Morhauptin, the young Geiserlin, Paul Glaser, [and others]. After this they had dispersed,

At this time his paramour had promised to provide him with money, and from time to time to take him to other witch-gatherings.

. . . Whenever he wished to ride forth [to the witch-sabbath] a black dog had come before his bed, which said to him that he must go with him, whereupon he had seated himself upon the dog and the dog had raised himself in the Devil's name and so had fared forth.

About two years ago he was taken to the electoral council-room, at the left hand as one goes in. Above at a table were seated the Chancellor, the Burgomaster Neydekher, Dr. George Haan, [and many others]. Since his eyes were not good, he could not recognize more persons.

More time for consideration was now given him. On July 7, the aforesaid Junius was again examined, to know what further had occurred to him to confess. He confesses that about two months ago, on the day after an execution was held, he was at a witch-dance at the Black Cross, where Beelzebub had shown himself to them all and said expressly to their faces that they must all be burned together on this spot, and had ridiculed and taunted those present. . . .

Of crimes. His paramour had immediately after his seduction demanded that he should make away with his younger son Hans Georg, and had given him for this purpose a gray powder; this, however, being too hard for him, he had made away with his horse, a brown, instead.

His paramour had also often spurred him on to kill his daughter, . . . and because he would not do this he had been maltreated with blows by the evil spirit.

Once at the suggestion of his paramour he had taken the holy wafer out of his mouth and given it to her. . . .

A week before his arrest as he was going to St. Martin's church the Devil met him on the way, in the form of a goat, and told him that he would soon be imprisoned, but that he should not trouble himself--he would soon set him free. Besides this, by, his soul's salvation, he knew nothing further; but what he had spoken was the pure truth on that he would stake his life. On August 6, 1628, there was read to the aforesaid Jnnius this his confession, which he then wholly ratified and confirmed, and was willing to stake his life upon it. And afterward he voluntarily confirmed the same before the court.

[So ended the trial of Junius, and he was accordingly burned at the stake. But it so happens that there is also preserved in Bamberg a letter, in quivering hand, secretly written by him to his daughter while in the midst of his trial (July 24, 1628):]

Many hundred thousand good-nights, dearly beloved daughter Veronica. Innocent have I come into prison, innocent have I been tortured, innocent must I die. For whoever comes into the witch prison must become a witch or be tortured until he invents something out of his head and--God pity him--bethinks him of something. I will tell you how it has gone with me. When I was the first time put to the torture, Dr. Braun, Dr. Kötzendörffer, and two strange doctors were there. Then Dr. Braun asks me, "Kinsman, how come you here?" I answer, "Through falsehood, through misfortune." "Hear, you," he says, "you are a witch; will you confess it voluntarily? If not, we'll bring in witnesses and the executioner for you." I said "I am no witch, I have a pure conscience in the matter; if there are a thousand witnesses, I am not anxious, but I'll gladly bear the witnesses." Now the chancellor's son was set before me . . . and afterward Hoppfen Elsa. She had seen me dance on Haupts-moor. . . . I answered: "I have never renounced God, and will never do it--God graciously keep me from it. I'll rather bear whatever I must." And then came also--God in highest Heaven have mercy--the executioner, and put the thumb-screws on me, both hands bound together, so that the blood ran out at the nails and everywhere, so that for four weeks I could not use my hands, as you can see from the writing. . . . Thereafter they first stripped me, bound my hands behind me, and drew me up in the torture. [32] Then I thought heaven and

---

[32] This torture of the strappado, which was that in most common use by the courts, consisted of a rope, attached to the hands of the prisoner (bound behind his back) and carried over a pulley at the ceiling. By this he was drawn

earth were at an end; eight times did they draw me up and let me fall again, so that I suffered terrible agony. . . .

And this happened on Friday, June 30, and with God's help I had to bear the torture. . . . When at last the executioner led me back into the prison, he said to me: "Sir, I beg you, for God's sake confess something, whether it be true or not. Invent something, for you cannot endure the torture which you will he put to; and, even if you bear it all, yet you will not escape, not even if you were ail earl, but one torture will follow after another until you say you are a witch. Not before that," he said, "will they let you go, as you may see by all their trials, for one is just like another." . . .

And so I begged, since I was in wretched plight, to be given one day for thought and a priest. The priest was refused me, but the time for thought was given. Now, my dear child, see in what hazard I stood and still stand. I must say that I am a witch, though I am not,--must now renounce God, though I have never done it before. Day and night I was deeply troubled, but at last there came to me a new idea. I would not be anxious, but, since I had been given no priest with whom I could take counsel, I would myself think of something and say it. It were surely better that I just say it with mouth and words, even though I had not really done it; and afterwards I would confess it to the priest, and let those answer for it who compel me to do it. . . . And so I made my confession, as follows; but it was all a lie.

Now follows, dear child, what I confessed in order to escape the great anguish and bitter torture, which it was impossible for me longer to bear.

[Here follows his confession, substantially as it is given in the minutes of his trial. But he adds:]

---

up and left hanging. To increase the pain, weights were attached to his feet or he was suddenly jerked up and let drop.

Then I had to tell what people I had seen [at the witch-sabbath]. I said that I had not recognized them. "You old rascal, I must set the executioner at you. Say--was not the Chancellor there?" So I said yes. "Who besides?" I had not recognized anybody. So be said: "Take one street after another; begin at the market, go out on one street and back on the next." I had to name several persons there. Then came the long street. [33] I knew nobody. Had to name eight persons there. Then the Zinkenwert--one person more. Then over the upper bridge to the Georgthor, on both sides. Knew nobody again

Did I know nobody in the castle--whoever it might be, I should speak without fear. And thus continuously they asked me on all the streets, though I could not and would not say more. So they gave me to the executioner, told him to strip me, shave me all over, and put me to the torture. "The rascal knows one on the market-place, is with him daily, and yet won't name him." By that they meant Dietmeyer: so I had to name him too.

Then I had to tell what crimes I had committed. I said nothing. . . "Draw the rascal up I" So I said that I was to kill my children, but I had killed a horse instead. It did not help. I had also taken a sacred wafer, and had desecrated it. When I had said this, they left me in peace.

Now, dear child, here you have all my confession, for which I must die. And they are sheer lies and made-up things, so help me God. For all this I was forced to say through fear of the torture which was threatened beyond what I had already endured. For they never leave off with the torture till one confesses something; be he never so good, he must be a witch, Nobody escapes, though he were an earl.

---

[33] *Die lange gasse*,"--the street is still known by that name.

Dear child, keep this letter secret so that people do not find it, else I shall be tortured most piteously and the jailers will be beheaded. So strictly is it forbidden. . . . Dear child, pay this man a dollar. . . . I have taken several days to write this: my hands are both lame. I am in a sad plight. . . .

Good night, for your father Johannes Junius will never see you more, July 24, 1628.

[And on the margin of the letter he adds:]

Dear child, six have confessed against me at once: the Chancellor, his son, Neudecker, Zaner, Hoffmaisters Ursel, and Hoppfen Els--all false, through compulsion, as they have all told me, and begged my forgiveness in God's name before they were executed. . . . They know nothing but good of me. They were forced to say it, just as I myself was. . . .

VII. THE WITCH-PERSECUTION AT WÜRZBURG.

From *Codex german.* 1254 of the Munich library, as printed by Leitschuh, *Beiträge zur Geschichte des Hexenwesens in Franken.*

In August, 1629, the Chancellor of the Prince-Bishop of Würzburg thus wrote (in German) to a friend:

As to the affair of the witches, which Your Grace thinks brought to an end before this, it has started up afresh, and no words can do justice to it. Ah, the woe and the misery of it--there are still four hundred in the city, high and low, of every rank and sex, nay, even clerics, so strongly accused that they may be arrested at any hour. It is true that, of the people of my Gracious Prince here, some out of all offices and faculties must be executed: clerics, electoral councilors and doctors, city officials, court assessors, several of whom Your Grace knows. There are law students to be arrested. The Prince-Bishop has over forty students who are soon to be pastors; among them thirteen or fourteen are said to be witches. A few days ago a Dean was arrested; two others who were summoned have fled. The notary of our Church consistory, a very learned man, was yesterday arrested and put to the torture. In a word, a third part of the city is surely involved. The richest, most attractive, most prominent, of the clergy are already executed. A week ago a maiden of nineteen was executed, of whom it is everywhere said that she was the fairest in the whole city, and was held by everybody a girl of singular modesty and purity. She will be followed by seven or eight others of the best and most attractive persons. . . . And thus many are put to death for renouncing God and being at the witch-dances, against whom nobody has ever else spoken a word.

To conclude this wretched matter, there are children of three and four years, to the number of three hundred, who are said to have had intercourse with the Devil. I have seen put to death children of seven, promising students of ten, twelve, fourteen, and fifteen.

Of the nobles--but I cannot and must not write more of this misery. There are persons of yet higher rank, whom you know, and would marvel to hear of, nay, would scarcely believe it; let justice be done . . .

P. S.--Though there are many wonderful and terrible things happening, it is beyond doubt that, at a place called the Fraw-Rengberg, the Devil in person, with eight thousand of his followers, held an assembly and celebrated mass before them all, administering to his audience (that is, the witches) turnip-rinds and parings in place of the Holy Eucharist. There took place not only foul but most horrible and hideous blasphemies, whereof I shudder to write. It is also true that they all vowed not to be enrolled in the Book of Life, but all agreed to be inscribed by a notary who is well known to me and my colleagues. We hope, too, that the book in which they are enrolled will yet be found, and there is no little search being made for it.

VIII. THE METHODS OF THE

WITCH-PERSECUTIONS.

It was at this very time, and probably at Würzburg during the persecution just above described, that the noble Jesuit poet, Friedrich Spee, was made the confessor of those sentenced to death for witchcraft and was thus inspired to write (though anonymously) the book whose eloquent protest gave the persecution throughout Europe its first effective check. Not till long afterward did the philosopher Leibnitz reveal its authorship, on the authority of his friend Johann Philipp von Schönborn, Archbishop of Mainz, who in his youth at Würzburg had known and loved Father Spee and had learned from him the whole story in answer to a question as to the young father's whitened hair. The last of the fifty-one doubts into which Spee's *Cautio criminalis* (Rinteln, 1631) is divided runs thus (pp. 378-392):

What, now, is the outline and method of the trials against witches to-day in general use?--a thing worthy Germany's consideration.

I answer: . . .

1. Incredible among us Germans and especially (I blush to say it) among Catholics are the popular superstition, envy, calumnies, backbitings, insinuations, and the like, which, being neither punished by the magistrates nor refuted by the pulpit, first stir up suspicion of witchcraft. All the divine judgements which God has threatened in Holy Writ are now ascribed to witches. No longer do God or nature do aught, but witches everything.

2. Hence it comes that all at once everybody is clamoring that the magistrates proceed against the witches--those witches whom only their own clamor has made seem so many.

3. Princes, therefore, bid their judges and counselors to begin proceedings against the witches.

4. These at first do not know where to begin, since they have no testimony or proofs, and since their conscience clearly tells them that they ought not to proceed in this rashly.

5. Meanwhile they are a second time and a third admonished to proceed. The multitude clamors that there is something suspicious in this delay; and the same suspicion is, by one busybody or another, instilled into the ear of the princes.

6. To offend these, however, and not to defer at once to their wishes, is in Germany a serious matter: most men, and even clergymen, approve with zeal whatever is but pleasing to the princes, not heeding by whom these (however good by nature) are often instigated.

7. At last, therefore, the Judges yield to their wishes, and in some way contrive at length a starting-point for the trials.

8. Or, if they still hold out and dread to touch the ticklish matter, there is sent to them a commissioner [*Inquisitor*] specially deputed for this. And, even if he brings to his task something of inexperience or of haste, as is wont to happen in things human, this takes on in this field another color and name, and is counted only zeal for justice. This zeal for justice is no whit diminished by the prospect of gain, especially in the case of a commissioner of slender means and avaricious, with a large family, when there is granted him as salary so many dollars per head for each witch burned, besides the fees and assessments which he is allowed to extort at will from the peasants.

9. If now some utterance of a demoniac [34] or some malign and idle rumor then current (for proof of the scandal is never asked) points especially to some poor and helpless Gaia, [35] she is the first to suffer.

10. And yet, lest it appear that she is indicted on the basis of rumor alone, without other proofs, as the phrase goes, lo a certain presumption is at once obtained against her by posing the following dilemma: Either Gaia has led a bad and improper life, or she has led a good proper one. If a bad one, then, say they, the proof is cogent against her; for from malice to malice the presumption is strong. If, however, she has led a good one, this also is none the less a proof; for thus, they say, are witches wont to cloak themselves and try to seem especially proper.

11. Therefore it is ordered that Gaia be haled away to prison. And lo now a new proof is gained against her by this other dilemma: Either she then shows fear or she does not show it. If she does show it (hearing forsooth of the grievous tortures wont to be used in this matter), this is of itself a proof; for conscience, they say, accuses her. If she does not show it (trusting forsooth in her innocence), this too is a proof; for it is most characteristic of witches, they say, to pretend themselves peculiarly innocent and wear a bold front.

12. Lest, however, further proofs against her should be lacking, the Commissioner has his own creatures, often depraved and notorious, who question into all her past life. This, of course, cannot be done without coming upon some saying or doing of hers which evil-minded men can easily twist or distort into ground for suspicion of witchcraft.

---

[34] i. e., of course, an insane person.
[35] i. e., woman. Gaia was the name used for a female culprit by the Roman law--like the John Doe or Richard Roe of our own legal parlance.

If, too, there are any who have borne her ill will, these, having now a fine opportunity to do her harm, bring against her such charges as it may please them to devise; and on every side there is a clamor that the evidence is heavy against her.

14. And so, as soon as possible, she is hurried to the torture, if indeed she be not subjected to it on the very day of her arrest, as often happens.

15. For in these trials there is granted to nobody an advocate or any means of fair defense, for the cry is that the crime is an excepted one, [36] and whoever ventures to defend the prisoner is brought into suspicion of the crime--as are all those who dare to utter a protest in these cases and to urge the judges to caution; for they are forthwith dubbed patrons of the witches. Thus all mouths are closed and all pens blunted, lest they speak or write.

16. In general, however, that it may not seem that no opportunity of defense has been given to Gaia, she is brought out and the proofs are first read before her and examined--if examine it can be called.

17. But, even though she then denies these and satisfactorily makes answer to each, this is neither paid attention to nor even noted down: all the proofs retain their force and value, however perfect her answer to them. She is only ordered back into prison, there to bethink herself more carefully whether she will persist in her obstinacy--for, since she has denied her guilt, she is obstinate.

18. When she has bethought herself, she is next day brought out again, and there is read to her the sentence of torture--just as if

---

[36] *Crimina excepta* were those in which, by reason of their enormity, all restraints upon procedure were suspended. Such were treason, and, by analogy, treason against heaven--heresy, that is, and especially witchcraft. In dealing with the latter an added ground for severity was found in the belief that the Devil might aid supernaturally his allies.

she had before answered nothing to the charges, and refuted nothing.

19. Before she is tortured, however, she is led aside by the executioner, and, lest she may by magical means have fortified herself against pain, she is searched, her whole body being shaved, although up to this time nothing of the sort was ever found.

21. Then, when Gaia has thus been searched and shaved, she is tortured that she may confess the truth, that is to say, that she may simply declare herself guilty; for whatever else she may say will not be the truth and cannot be.

22. She is, however, tortured with the torture of the first degree, i. e., the less severe. This is to be understood thus: that, although in itself it is exceeding severe, yet, compared with others to follow, it is lighter. Wherefore, if she confesses, they say and noise it abroad that she has confessed without torture.

23. Now, what prince or other dignitary who bears this can doubt that she is most certainly guilty who thus voluntarily without torture confesses her guilt?

24. Without any scruples, therefore, after this confession she s executed. Yet she would have been executed, nevertheless, even though she had not confessed; for, when once a beginning has been made with the torture, the die is already cast--she cannot escape, she must die.

25. So, whether she confesses or does not confess, the result is the same. If she confesses, the thing is clear, for, as I have said and as is self-evident, she is executed: all recantation is in vain, as I have shown above. If she does not confess, the torture is repeated-twice, thrice, four times: anything one pleases is permissible, for in an excepted crime there is no limit of duration or severity or repetition of the tortures. As to this, think the judges, no sin is

possible which can be brought up before the tribunal of conscience. [37]

26. If now Gaia, no matter how many times tortured, has not yet broken silence if she contorts her features under the pain, if she loses consciousness, or the like, then they cry that she is laughing or has bewitched herself into taciturnity,[38] and hence deserves to be burned alive, as lately has been done to some who though several times tortured would not confess.

27. And then they say--even clergymen and confessors--that she died obstinate and impenitent, that she would not be converted or desert her paramour, [39] but kept rather her faith with him.

28. If, however, it chances that under so many tortures one dies, they say that her neck has been broken by the Devil.

29. Wherefore justly, forsooth, the corpse is dragged out by the executioner and buried under the gallows.

30. But if, on the other hand, Gaia does not die and some exceptionally scrupulous judge hesitates to torture her further without fresh proofs or to burn her without a confession, she is kept in prison and more harshly fettered, and there lies for perhaps an entire year to rot until she is subdued.

31. For it is never possible to clear herself by withstanding and thus to wash away the aspersion of crime, as is the intention of the laws. It would be a disgrace to her examiners if when once arrested she should thus go free. Guilty must she be, by fair means or foul, whom they have once but thrown into bonds.

---

[37] i. e., which can be inquired into by the priest in the confessional.

[38] *Uti maleficio tacturnitatis*, i. e., by witchcraft makes herself incapable of confession.

[39] i. e., of course, the Devil.

32. Meanwhile, both then and earlier, they send to her ignorant and headstrong priests, more importunate than the executioners themselves. It is the business of these to harass in every wise the wretched creature to such a degree that, whether truly or not, she will at last confess herself guilty; unless she does so, they declare, she simply cannot be saved, nor share in the sacraments.

33. The greatest care is taken lest there be admitted to her priests more thoughtful and learned, who have aught of insight or kindliness; as also that nobody visits her prison who might give her counsel or inform the ruling princes. For there is nothing so much dreaded by any of them as that in some way the innocence of any of the accused should be brought to light. . . .

34. In the meantime, while Gaia, as I have said, is still held in prison, and is tormented by those whom it least behooves, there are not wanting to her industrious judges clever devices by which they not only find new proofs against Gaia, but by which moreover they so convict her to her face (an 't please the gods!) that by the advice of some university faculty [40] she is then at last pronounced to deserve burning alive. . . .

35. Some, however, to leave no stone unturned, order Gaia to be exorcised and transferred to a new place, and then to be tortured again, in the hope that by this exorcism and change of place the bewitchment of taciturnity may perhaps be broken. But, if not even this succeeds, then at last they commit her alive to the flames. Now, in Heaven's name, I would like to know, since both she who confesses and she who does not perish alike, what way of escape is there for any, however innocent? O unhappy Gaia, why hast thou rashly hoped? why hast thou not, at first entering prison, declared thyself guilty? why, O foolish woman and mad, wilt thou die so many times when thou mightst die but once?

---

[40] It was sometimes the juristic, sometimes the theologic, faculty of a university which was called on for such advice, the crime of witchcraft being subject to both secular and ecclesiastical jurisdiction.

Follow my counsel, and before all pain declare thyself guilty and die. Thou wilt not escape; for this were a disgrace to the zeal of Germany.

36. If, now, any under stress of pain has once falsely declared herself guilty, her wretched plight beggars description. For not only is there in general no door for her escape, but she is also compelled to accuse others, of whom she knows no ill, and whose names are not seldom suggested to her by her examiners or by the executioner, or of whom she has heard as suspected or accused or already once arrested and released. These in their turn are forced to accuse others, and these still others, and so it goes on: who can help seeing that it must go on without end?

37. Wherefore the judges themselves are obliged at last either to break off the trials and so condemn their own work or else to burn their own folk, aye themselves and everybody: for on all soon or late false accusations fall, and, if only followed by the torture, all are proved guilty.

38. And so at last those are brought into question who at the outset most loudly clamored for the constant feeding of the flames; for they rashly failed to foresee that their turn, too, must inevitably come--and by a just verdict of Heaven, since with their pestilent tongues they created us so many witches and sent so many innocent to the flames,

39. But now gradually many of the wiser and more learned begin to take notice of it, and, as if aroused from deep sleep, to open their eyes and slowly and cautiously to bestir themselves. . . .

46. From all which there follows this corollary, worthy to be noted in red ink: that, if only the trials be steadily pushed on with, there is nobody in our day, of whatsoever sex, fortune, rank, or dignity, who is safe, if he have but an enemy and slanderer to bring him into suspicion of witchcraft. . . .

54

IX. SELECT BIBLIOGRAPHY.

There are few subjects on which so much has been written, yet so little that is serious in aim and scholarly in method. An idea of the literature as a whole may be gained from a paper on "The Literature of Witchcraft," contributed by the present editor to the Papers of the American Historical Association for 1890, and from Dr. Justin Winsor's "The Literature of Witchcraft in New England," in the Proceedings of the American Antiquarian Society for 1895. The best survey, in English, of the whole subject is still the chapter "Magic and Witchcraft" in Mr. Lecky's "History of the Rise and Influence of the Spirit of Rationalism in Europe." Mr. Lea's "History of the Inquisition in the Middle Ages" has precious chapters on "Sorcery and Occult Arts" and on "Witchcraft." Admirable for its insight is James Russell Lowell's essay on "Witchcraft" (in his "Among my Books"). Of the monographs the best of the more comprehensive are:

Soldan: Geschichte der Hexenprozesse. Neu bearbeitet von H. Heppe. 2 vols. Stuttgart, 1880.
Long the standard history of the witch-persecutions.

Hansen: Zauberwahn, Inquisition und Hexenprozess im Mittelalter und die Entstehung der grossen Hexenverfolgung. München, 1900.
The most thorough study of the rise of witch-persecution in Christendom. For the period prior to 1540 it supplants all else. Added as *Quellen Und Untersuchungen* (Bonn, 1901) is a priceless collection of sources.

Wright: Narratives of Sorcery and Magic. 2 vols. London, 1851. (I vol. New York, 1852.).
Written to entertain, and with little attempt at exhaustiveness, but the work of a true scholar. It is episodical in treatment and gives especial attention to the persecution in lands of English speech.

Baissac: Les Grands Jours de la Sorcellerie. Paris, 1890.
The best of the French histories of the subject. It gives most
attention to France. An earlier book of Baissac's, *Le Diable* (Paris,
1882), is also of value for this study.

**Diefenbach: Der Hexenwahn vor und nach der Glaubensspaltung
in Deutschland**. Mainz, 1886.
A study, by a Catholic apologist, of the share of the rival faiths in
the persecution. Directed in part against Soldan. An abler and
more thorough treatment from the Catholic side is now to be
found, however, in the eighth volume of Janssen's *Geschichte des
deutschen Volkes* (Freiburg, 1894).

Längin: Religion und Hexenprozess. Leipzig, 1888.
From a Protestant point of view. In part an answer to Diefenbach.

Michelet: La Sorcière. Paris, 1862.
An eloquent book, by a brilliant scholar; but a rhapsody rather
than a history, and as full of fancy as of fact. There is an English
translation (London, 1863).

Upham: Salem Witchcraft. 2 vols. Boston, 1867.
The standard work upon the most notable of American witch-
persecutions. It may be supplemented by Drake's *Annals of
Witchcraft in New England and elsewhere in the United States*
(Boston, 1869).

Roskoff: Geschichte des Teufels. 2 vols. Leipzig, 1869.
Best for the history of the Devil in his relation to witchcraft. Of
value, but dealing less with the witch persecution, are also
Conway's *Demonology and Devil-lore* (London, and New York,
1879) and Graf's *Il Diavolo* (Milan, 1889).

Binz: Doctor Johann Weyer. Bonn, 1885. 2d ed., enlarged, Berlin,
1896.
A scholarly biography of the first great opponent of witch-

persecution, with excellent sketches of his opponents and of his followers in this humane struggle.